CHANGE FOR GOOD

LIFE HACK 101

The Proven Strategies To Get You To Where You Want to Go In Life

Mabel Craig

Table of Contents

Chapter 1: How A Daily To-Do List Will Change Your Life 6
Chapter 2: Having A Balanced Lif 9
Chapter 3: Hitting Rock Bottom 12
Chapter 4: Don't Make Life Harder Than It Needs To Be 16
Chapter 5: Develop Mental Toughness In The Face of Adversity 20
Chapter 6: Discovering Your Strenghts and Weaknesses 23
Chapter 7: Don't Wait Another Second Live To Live Your Dreams ... 26
Chapter 8: Going Through Tough Times Is Part of The Journey 30
Chapter 9: 5 Tips to Doing Unique and Meaningful Work 33
Chapter 10: Eduaction and Experience- You Two Best Friends 37
Chapter 11: Choose Getting into Nature for Better Mood and Happiness 41
Chapter 12: Beginning In A New Stage Life 44
Chapter 13: 5 Tips to Doing Unique and Meaningful Work 48
Chapter 14: Move Towards the Next Thing, Not Away From the Last Thing 52
Chapter 15: 6 Concerning Effects of Mood On Your Life 55
Chapter 16: 6 Habits of Self-Love 60
Chapter 17: 6 Steps To Focus On Growth 65
Chapter 18: 6 Steps To Get Out of Your Comfort Zone 70
Chapter 19: 8 Ways To Change Your Body Language To Attract Success 76
Chapter 20: 6 Ways To Adopt A Better Lifestyle For Long-Term Success 81
Chapter 21: 6 Ways To transform Your Thinking 86
Chapter 22: 8 Habits That Can Make You Happy 90
Chapter 23: How To Trick Yourself Into Doing Anything 96
Chapter 24: Being Authentic 99
Chapter 25: Confidence: The Art of Humble-Pride 101

Chapter 26: Deal With Your Feras Now 103
Chapter 27: 4 Ways to Deal with Feelings of Inferiority When Comparing to Others 107
Chapter 28: Being Consistent, Not Perfect 110
Chapter 29: Be Motivated by Challenge 113
Chapter 30: Believe in Yourself 116

Chapter 1:

How A Daily To-Do List Will Change Your Life

To-do lists are generally underrated for a variety of reasons, and that's why we're giving you this article to go over some of the ways they can be useful to you as a professional, as well as a business owner. It's not likely that anyone within the sound of my voice has never used a to-do list at some point.

Meanwhile, many professionals don't regularly use them, depriving themselves of a simple tool that can help them be much more productive and keep everything in order.

Here's why you need to start using lists.

It Helps You to Effectively Prioritize Tasks

When running a business, your day can quickly get away from you if you don't have it mapped out. With so many things that need attention, high volumes of customers, various requests throughout the day, and internal problems, you have to be an uncommonly organized type of person to keep track of all of it without writing it down.

And that's the whole point. It's not that you aren't capable of doing everything your job requires, it's just that you need a written reference to look at so that nothing is missed. When you've got a list for yourself to reference throughout the day, week, or even further, one important benefit of this is that it gives you the ability to lay out tasks in a specific order. That is, you can lay out the plan in an order from toughest to easiest, most time-consuming to least, or any other order that keeps your priorities straight.

It's mainly about <u>making the best use of your time</u>. Some things need to get done first due to deadlines, and some things need to be done at a specific time because they will take longer, which tasks will need a sufficient block of time that you might only have available at certain times of the day.

More Easily See the Progress Of Your Work

Part of the advantage of seeing your work progress is that you can perpetually learn if you need to reorder your priorities because if the more important work isn't getting done, then you probably need to move those jobs up on your list. Not only that but you may not have a full appreciation for just how satisfying it is to cross items off of a to-do list as you're performing your work, no matter what that work is.

This is especially true when you cross off the more challenging items. These to-do lists are just not valued nearly as much as they should be, which is probably a large part of the reason why people don't feel like it's all that important to use them. It's extremely good for a business owner, psychologically, to participate in physically crossing things off a to-do list, considering how stressful it can be when you're looking at everything you need to get done.

Naturally, this isn't much help to you if you don't get tasks done, so you can cross them off, which is good because it will motivate you more to complete tasks when you see all of them right in front of you.

Having a record of everything you've done, even down to a daily basis, is great for a reference because, in the future, you can look back at your records and see where you're at. Not only is it satisfying to see how much you've accomplished, but you'll also see where you're falling short and need to improve productivity.

Chapter 2:

Having a Balanced Life

Today we're going to talk about how and why you should strive to achieve a balanced life. A balance between work, play, family, friends, and just time alone to yourself.

We all tend to lead busy lives. At some points we shift our entire focus onto something at the expense of other areas that are equally important.

I remember the time when I just got a new office space. I was so excited to work that i spent almost 95% of the week at the office. I couldn't for the life of me figured why i was so addicted to going to the office that I failed to see I was neglecting my family, my friends, my relationships. Soon after the novelty effect wore off, i found myself burnt out, distant from my friends and family, and sadly also found myself in a strained relationship.

This distance was created by me and me alone. I had forgotten what my priorities were. I hadn't realized that I had thrown my life completely off balance. I found myself missing the time I spent with my family and friends. And I found myself having to repair a strained relationship due to my lack of care and concern for the other party.

What you think is right in the moment, to focus on something exclusively at the expense of all else, may seem enticing. It may seem like there is nothing wrong with it. But dig deeper and check to make sure it is truly worth the sacrifice you are willing to make in other areas of your life.

It is easy for us to fall into the trap of wanting to make more money, wanting to work harder, to be career driven and all that. But what is the point in having more money if you don't have anyone to spend in on or spend it with? What's the point in having a nice car or a nice designer handbag if you don't have anyone to show it to?

Creating balance in our lives is a choice. We have the choice to carve out time in our schedule for the things that truly matter. Only when we know how to prioritize our day, our week, our month, can we truly find consistency and stability in our lives.

I know some people might say disagree with what I am sharing with you all today, but this is coming from my personal life experience. It was only after realizing that I had broken down all the things I had worked so hard to build prior to this new work venture, that I started to see the bigger picture again.

That I didn't want to go down this path and find myself 30 years later regretting that I had not spent time with my family before they passed away, that I was all alone in this world without someone I can lean my shoulder on to walk this journey with me, that I didn't have any friends that I could call up on a Tuesday afternoon to have lunch with me because everyone thought of me as a flaker who didn't prioritize them in the their lives before.

Choose the kind of life you want for yourself. If what I have to say resonates with you, start writing down the things that you know you have not been paying much attention to lately because of something else that you chose to do. Whether it be your lover, your friends, a hobby, a passion project, whatever it may be. Start doing it again. The time to create balance is now.

Chapter 3:

Hitting Rock Bottom

Today we're going to talk about a topic that I hope none of you will have to experience at any point in your lives. It can be a devastating and painful experience and I don't wish it on my worst enemy, but if this happens to be you, I hope that in today's video I can help you get out of the depths and into the light again.

First of all, I'm not going to waste any more time but just tell you that hitting rock bottom could be your blessing in disguise. You see when we hit rock bottom, the only reason that we know we are there is because we have become aware and have admitted to ourselves that there is no way lower that we can go. That we know deep in our hearts that things just cannot get any worse than this. And that revelation can be enlightening. Enlightening in the sense that by simple law of physics, the worse that can happen moving forward is either you move sideways, or up. When you have nothing more left to lose, you can be free to try and do everything in your power to get back up again.

For a lot of us who have led pretty comfortable lives, sometimes it feels like we are living in a bubble. We end up drifting through life on the comforts of our merits that we fail to stop learning and growing as people. We become so jaded about everything that life becomes bland.

We stop trying to be better, we stop trying to care, and we that in itself could be poison. It is like a frog getting boiled gradually, we don't notice it until it is too late, and we are cooked. We are in fact slowly dying and fading into irrelevance.

But when you are at rock bottom, you become painfully aware of everything. Painfully aware of maybe your failed relationships, the things you did and maybe the people you hurt that have led you to this point. You become aware that you need to change yourself first, that everything starts with growing and learning again from scratch, like a baby learning how to walk again. And that could be a very rewarding time in your life when you become virtually fearless to try and do anything in your power to get back on your feet again.

Of course, all this has to come from you. That you have to make the decision that things will never stay the same again. That you will learn from your mistakes and do the right things. When you've hit rock bottom, you can slowly begin the climb one step at a time.

Start by defining the first and most important thing that you cannot live without in life. If family means the most to you, reach out to them. Find comfort and shelter in them and see if they are able to provide you with any sort of assistance while you work on your life again. I always believe that if family is the most important thing, and that people you call family will be there with you till the very end. If family is not available to you, make it a priority to start growing a family. Family doesn't mean you have to have blood relations. Family is whoever you can rely on in your darkest times. Family is people who will accept you and love you for who you are in spite of your shortcomings. Family is people that will help nurture and get you back on your own two feet again. If you don't have family, go get one.

If hitting rock bottom to you means that you feel lost in life, in your career and finance, that you maybe lost your businesses and are dealing with the aftermath, maybe your first priority is to simply find a simple part time job that can occupy your time and keep you sustained while you figure out what to do next. Sometimes all we need is a little break to clear our heads and to start afresh again. Nothing ever stays the same. Things will get better. But don't fall into the trap of ruminating on your losses as it can be very destructive on your mental health. The past has already happened, and you cannot take it back. Take stock of the reasons and don't make the same mistakes again in your career and you will be absolutely fine.

If you feel like you've hit rock bottom because of a failed marriage or relationship, whether it be something you did or your partner did, I know this can be incredibly painful and it feels like you've spent all your time with someone with nothing to show for it but wasted time and energy, but know that things like that happen and that it is perfectly normal. Humans are flawed and we all make mistakes. So yes, it is okay to morn over the loss of the relationship and feel like you can't sink any lower, but don't lose faith as you will find someone again.

If hitting rock bottom is the result of you being ostracized by people around you for not being a good person, where you maybe have lost all the relationships in your life because of something you did, I'm sure you know the first step to do is to accept that you need to change. Don't look to someone else to blame but look inwards instead. Find time where you can go away on your way to reflect on what went wrong. Start going through the things that people were unhappy with you about and start looking for ways to improve yourself. If you need help, I am here for you. If not, maybe you might want to seek some professional help as well to dig a little deeper and to help guide you along a better path.

Hitting rock bottom is not a fun thing, and I don't want to claim that I know every nuance and feeling of what it means to get there, but I did feel like that once when my business failed on me and I made the decision that I could only go up from here. I started to pour all my time and energy into proving to myself that I will succeed no matter what and that I will not sit idly by and feel sorry for myself. It was a quite a journey, but I came out of it stronger than before and realized that I was more resourceful than I originally thought.

So, I challenge each and everyone of you who feels like you've hit the bottom to not be afraid of taking action once again. To be fearless and just take that next right step forward no matter what. And I hope to see you on the top of the mountain in time to come.

Chapter 4:

Don't Make Life Harder Than It Needs To Be

Today we're going to talk about a topic that I hope will inspire you to make better decisions and to take things more lightly. As we go through this journey of life together, and as we get older, we soon find ourselves with more challenges that we need to face, more problems that we need to solve, and more responsibilities that we need to take on as an adult. In each phase of life, the bar gets set higher for us. When we are young, our troubles mostly revolve around school and education. For most of us we don't have to worry much about making money or trying to provide for a family, although I know that some of you who come from lesser well off families might have had to start doing a lot earlier. And to you i commend you greatly. For the rest of us we deal with problems with early teenage dating, body image, puberty, grades, and so on. It is only until we graduate from university do we face the harsh reality of the real world. Of being a working adult. It is only then are we really forced to grow up. To face nasty colleagues, bosses, customers, you name it. And that is only just the beginning.

Life starts to get more complicated for many of us when we start to realize that we have to manage our own finances now. When our parents stop giving us money and that we only have ourselves to rely on to survive. Suddenly reality hits us like a truck. We realise that making our own money becomes our primary focus and that we may not have much else to rely on. We take on loans, mortgages, credit card debts, and it seems to never really end. For many of us, we may end up in a rat race that we can't get out of because of the payments and loans that we have already ended up committing to. The things we buy have a direct impact on the obligations that have to maintain.

Next, we have to worry about finding a partner, marriage, starting a family, buying a house, providing for your kids, setting aside money for their growth, college fund, the list goes on and on.

Do you feel overwhelmed with this summary of the first maybe one-third of your life? The reality is that that is probably the exact timeline that most of us will eventually go through. The next phase of life requires us to keep up the payments, to go to our jobs, to keep making that dough to sustain our family. We may have to also make enough money to pay for tuition fees, holidays, gifts, payments to parents, and whatever other commitments that we might have. And this might go on until we reach 60, when two-thirds of our lives are already behind us.

Life as you can see, without any external help, is already complicated enough. If you didn't already know by now, life isn't easy. Life is full of challenges, obligations, obstacles, commitments, and this is without any unforeseen events that might happen... Medical or family wise.

With all this in mind, why do we want to make life harder than it already is?

Every additional decision that you make on top of this list will only add to your burden, if it is not the right one, and every person that you add into your life that is negative will only bring the experience much less enjoyable.

To make life easier for you and your soul, I recommend that you choose each step wisely. Choose carefully the partner that you intend to spend your life with, choose wisely the people that you choose to spend your time with, choose wisely the food that you put in your body, and choose wisely the life that you wish to lead.

Be absolutely clear on the vision that you have for your life because it ain't easy.

Another thing to make your life much less complicated is to put less pressure on yourself. I believe that you don't need to start comparing your life with others because everyone is on their own journey. Don't chase the fancy houses and cars that your friends have just because they have them. Everyone is different and everyone's priorities might be different as well. They might pride having a luxury car over spending on other areas of life, which might differ from the interests that you might have. Comparison will only most certainly lead you to chase a life that you might not even want to attain. And you might lose your sleep and mind trying to match up to your peers. Focus on yourself instead and on exactly what you want out of life, and it will definitely be enough.

I challenge each and everyone of you to have a clear set of priorities for yourself. And once you have done so and are working towards those goals, be contented about it. Don't change the goalpost just because your friends say you must, or because you are jealous of what they have. Be satisfied in your own path and life will reward you with happiness as well.

Chapter 5:

Develop Mental Toughness In The Face of Adversity

The drawback of this technological revolution that we live in is that we have created a weaker generation, a weaker society. We need everything to be perfect, to be exactly the way we want it to be.

We can't bear a single change in our routines. We can't handle a single harmless task that might test us in any way possible. We can't forgive anyone's mistake, but we want all our blunders to be erased.

We can't handle the fact that life is always a step ahead of us. And if something bad happens, we try to mask it. We never try to actually deal with the problems, rather keep them at bay as long as we can.

We are so afraid of trying the do the things that would matter, but we become the wisest when we mock or advise someone else.

We are never truly prepared for the hard times. We are always in a constant fight with our own minds, neglecting reality and creating a false scenario where everything is alright. It is not Alright!

We are living in a time where everyone is in search of greatness. There are more and more people coming into this world every day and the competition is getting harder than it ever was. The day will come when we would have to fight for even the basic necessities of life.

The day might come when we will fail at almost everything we are doing right now. What will we do then?

Life gives us second chances, but those chances require us to be stronger. Those chances want us to first create some chances beforehand before we go forward with the grand scheme.

Chances present themselves to the people who are in the constant struggle to live every minute as if it were their last.

If someone was to ask you to join them for a morning run, you might be enthusiastic for one day. You will wake up at five in the morning, gear up, and go for 10 miles for the first day. On the second day, you will go for it again. A week later you will take a break for a day. A month later you might get a treadmill because you feel more comfortable running in your home rather than going out in the cold mornings. But eventually, you will stop doing it.

All of this is because you are not ready to get out of your comfort zone or not ready to commit for long enough to achieve what you started for.

Learn to say 'No' to 'No'. The day you start saying no to everything that will keep you in your warm cozy bed, is the day you will finally realize what you will achieve that day.

Life will always be hard on you, but you can join the league of successful beings if you stay true to your cause and keep pushing and digging till you finally find the gem of your choice.

Chapter 6:
Discovering Your Strengths and Weaknesses

Today we're going to talk about a very simple yet important topic that hopefully brings about some self-discovery about who you really are. By the end of this video, I wish to help you find out what areas you are weak at so that maybe you could work on those, and what your strengths are so that you can play to them and lean into them more for greater results in your career and life in general.

We should all learn to accept our flaws as much as we embrace our strengths. And we have to remember that each of us are unique, and we excel in different areas. Some of us are more artistic, some visionary, some analytical, some hardworking, some lazy, what matters is that we make these qualities work for us in our own special way.

Let's start by identifying your weaknesses. For those of you that have watched enough of my videos, you would know that i encourage all of you to take a pen to write things down. So let's go through this exercise real quick. Think of a few things that people have told you that you needed to work on, be it from your teachers, your friends, your family, or whoever it may be.

How many of these weaknesses would you rate as significantly important that it would affect your life in a drastic way if you did not rectify it? I want you to put them at the top of your list. Next spend some time to reflect and look in the mirror. Be honest with yourself and identify the areas about yourself that you know needs some work.

Now I want you to take some time to identity your strengths. Repeat the process from above, what are the things people have told you about yourself that highlighted certain qualities about you? Whether that you're very outgoing, friendly, a great singer, a good team player, very diligent. I want you to write as many of these down as you can. No matter how big or small these strengths are, I want you to write down as many as you can.

Now I want you to also place your 3 biggest strengths at the top of the list. As I believe these are the qualities that best represent who you are as a person.

Now that you've got these 2 lists. I want you to compare them. Which list is longer? the one with strengths or weaknesses? If you have more weaknesses, that's okay, it just means that there is more room for improvement. If you have more strengths, that's good.

What we are going to do with this list now is to now make it a mission to improve our weaknesses and play heavily into our strengths for the foreseeable future. You see, our strengths are strengths for a reason, we are simply naturally good at it. Whether it be through genetics, or our personalities, or the way we have been influenced by the world. We should all try to showcase our strengths as much as we can. It is hard for me to say exactly what that is, but I believe that you will know how you maximize the use of your talent. Whether it be serving others, performing for others, or even doing specific focused tasks. Simply do more of it. Put yourself in more situations where you can practice these strengths. And keep building on it. It will take little effort but yield tremendous results.

As for your weaknesses, I want you to spend some time on the top 3 that you have listed so far. As these could be the areas that have been holding you back the most. Making improvements in these areas could be the breakthrough that you need to become a much better person and could see you achieving a greater level success than if you had just left them alone.

I challenge each and everyone of you to continually play to your strengths, sharpening them until they are sharp as a knife, while working on smoothening the rough edges of your weaknesses. So that they may balance out your best qualities.

Chapter 7:

Don't Wait Another Second To Live Your Dreams

We often think we must be ready to act, but the truth is we will never be ready while we wait.

We only become ready by walking the path, and battles are seldom won in ideal circumstances.

Money is not the real currency in life, the real currency is time and every second we wait is a second, we waste.

Your biggest motivator is the ticking clock and the impending reality that one day it will be too late.

Your biggest fear is getting to 80 and realizing you haven't lived, that you haven't done what you wanted in life because of fear.

True regret is a medicine none of us want to taste.

We must decide what we really want, set the bar high, go after it now and accept nothing less.

You deserve respect, but you will live what you expect, this life will pay you any price but it's up to you what you accept.

You must act now from where we are with what we have, right now, not tomorrow or next week, right now.

Take the first step, make the draft plan.

Find out what knowledge you need to make this dream a reality.

Taking action now towards the goal in mind is crucial, if we wait, we risk losing the drive to make things happen.

We can never be fully ready because we don't know what exactly is going to happen, a lot of it is learned along the way - especially if you're doing something brand new.

If not, reading what has been done before in your area will give you a good understanding of what might work.

Every second we spend thinking about, instead of acting towards our goal is wasted time.

You cannot afford to wait because if you do not act, someone else will, someone else could also be thinking what you're thinking and act first.

Those who wait for opportunity will wait in vain because opportunity must be created, first in the mind, then in the world.

We cannot see the vast opportunity that surrounds us unless we believe it is there, believe it is possible and act on that belief, at the time it arises.

The world is pliable, and opportunities do not wait for people to be ready. You must become ready on the road.

The obstacles you have to overcome on the move will mold you into the person you need to be to reach your biggest goals.

You must be patient, to be practitioners of who you believe you will be one day.

Getting into the mindset of whoever you want to be right now, because until you become that person in mind, you cannot in body.

As we start acting differently, different actions bring different results and if the new actions are positive and aimed at a certain goal, just like magic the world begins to transform for you, towards the life you wanted.

The leap of faith is acting now, feeling unready aiming for something that may seem unrealistic, but this is an essential leap and test to be overcome. As the days go on with the goal in mind, it will seem to become more likely, and you will feel more ready until it feels definite.

All things are possible but there will be required ingredients to your success you might not know yet, so the first step is to gain the knowledge required.

Once you begin to learn that knowledge you are on the road to your goal. Organization and optimization of your time will make it easier to be efficient.

If time is the real currency, are you getting good value for what you spend your time doing?

If not, is it not time you used some of your seconds working towards something phenomenal?

You only have so many, and it is losing value every day as we age, think about it.

We must create a sense of urgency because it is urgent if you want to succeed in an ever changing world.

If we wait our ideas, products and services may become irrelevant because new technology and innovation is always changing.

Our ideas are only viable when they come,

Strike while the iron is hot is good advice,

When the ambition and goal is strongest and clearest.

Clarity is essential when pursuing dreams and goals, every detail of your dream should be clear in your mind down to the sights, colours and smells.

When we think about our goal, we should feel it as if it's already here, and start acting like it is.

Dress talk and walk as if you are that person now.

Whatever our current circumstances everyone has the ability to build in their minds, set the goal then determine the first step.

If your circumstances are bad there are more steps, but there are steps.

Start from step one and walk in confidence always keeping the big dream in mind knowing that this can happen for you.

We have a waking mind and a subconscious mind.

The subconscious knows things we don't, it is responsible for our gut instinct, which always seems to be right so follow that.

Everyday listening to that voice, keeping a clear vision of your goal in your mind and confidently taking action towards it.

It's possible for you if you act,

But time is ticking.

Chapter 8:

Going Through Tough Times Is Part of The Journey

For someone going through tough times, for someone going through the same hardships, again and again, every day, you are trying but not getting used to all this.

Things never seem to get better, and you don't think you are just right there to get a hold of things. You think you will get them this time, but they always seem to be going a new way that you never planned.

It's alright! You are not the first one to think about things this way are you certainly won't be the last one.

You are not the first person to think that you will have different achievements this time. You are not the first person to think that you will achieve bigger goals this year. You are not the first person to fail at every corner after all that determination and grit.

Life always kicks us on the blindside, and most of us know what it feels like. But not all of us want to stay in the bed all day and feel sorry for ourselves for what happened before.

People always find a way to cope with the tragedies of life. And these people know the true purpose of life. They know the true definition of life. Wanna know what that is? It's the hard times that make you a harder more precious gem.

You can never possibly understand why it is happening to you because it is what it is and you can never set your back to reality.
The reality is that no one has ever lived a reasonable life without facing the hard times. And only the people who smiled back at these hard times had a happy ending in the end.

The only thing that makes us go through life with a smile in the hope of getting a big reward at the end of it all. Our lives aren't judged on the number of success stories we write, but with the techniques, we adapt to tackle the moments when life pushes us against a wall.

It won't always be your fault, but it might be your luck trying to test your limits. So why don't you show it?

Things will always go wrong in your life but that doesn't make it justifiable to put everything aside and start mourning and regretting your every mistake and every flaw. But it's time to start removing those flaws to minimize your mistakes and trying to be a perfect individual.

This is the journey to perfection that makes going through hard times justifiable. Because every stone that your pick and set aside is another hurdle being cleared for an easier road to the top.

What happens to you in life is just a glimpse of the reality, but what you do about those things in life is what living this life is actually about.

Always remember, you and your life are always like a plane. You both fly against the winds but never along it.

Chapter 9:

5 Tips to Doing Unique and Meaningful Work

When you think about meaningful work, you think about Mother Theresa or Princess Diana or maybe Peace Corp workers or school teachers and nurses. All of these are great and meaningful jobs. But, not everyone can raise money and attention to help get landmines cleared, nor can (or should) everyone try to teach second grade. And if blood makes you faint, nursing isn't a great idea for you either.

So, how can you make your job meaningful work, even when it's not directly making anyone's life better? These five suggestions will change your job from tedious work to meaningful work.

1. Look at the Big Picture

Why does your job exist? You could be an HR manager, a grocery store cashier, or a tech company CEO. Each of these jobs is necessary to make the world a better place.

Because this is no longer an agrarian society, you need the grocery store cashier to get food. CEOs of well-managed companies provide goods and services to the community and jobs with paychecks for many people. And HR managers can make people's lives much better by helping them progress in their careers, finding and providing the best benefits, and hiring great people.

If you just look at the tasks in front of you, you'll forget how you contribute to the community as a whole.

2. Treat Each Other With Kindness

A kind person can change everyone's day from drudgery to fun. Yes, work is still working, and sometimes it's hard, but working with the right people can make you look forward to working even if the job is hard work.

One man who worked for a brewery as a delivery man could have seen his job as hard work and struggle. After all, his job duty was to drive from restaurant to restaurant, carrying huge kegs of beer and taking out the old, empty ones. But the people in many restaurants cheered when the beer guy came in with the beer kegs. Their act of kindness changed his job from drudgery to one that he loved.

3. Work Hard

How does working hard make a job meaningful? Well, hard work often equals success. When you succeed in your job, you help others in your department succeed in their jobs. When your whole department succeeds, the company succeeds. That is pretty meaningful.

Additionally, hard work is easier than avoiding work. Think about it: when you have to worry if your boss knows how much time you're spending surfing the internet, that adds another layer of complexity to your job. When you're working hard all of the time, and your boss drops by, it's not a big deal.

When you keep on top of your work, you have lowered stress levels. Now, of course, some people are overburdened and cannot accomplish everything. You might start feeling like, "I can't get everything done, so why bother?" These feelings of stress and failure can pose a huge temptation, but don't give in. First of all, you'll start to feel like your job just isn't meaningful—it's just work. Second, that adds additional stress on top of your head.

What you do instead is go to your boss and say directly, "I have five tasks on my plate right now. I can do four effectively, or I can do a lousy job on all five. Which would you prefer?" or "I have five tasks on my plate right now. I only have time to get three of them done. Which two should I skip?"

4. Look Outside of Your Job

Does your meaningful work have to be your day job? Of course not. Sometimes your day job can fund your meaningful work. Work-life balance means having a life. Whether it's through your family, church, charity, art, or whatever is important to you, you need a paycheck to support that.

You don't have to fulfill all of your needs through your paid job. You don't even need to feel guilty that you're working for a large corporation rather than a small non-profit. It's not bad to earn money. You find your meaning in how you can spend that money.

5. Consider Changing Jobs

If you just can't see how your current job is meaningful, and you can't figure out a way to make your job meaningful work, then perhaps it's time for you to move on. If your job doesn't bring you joy, doesn't allow you to support your family or essential charitable causes, and doesn't help the community, then maybe it's not the right job for you.

No one has a skill set that is so tiny and unique that there is only one job in the world that would suit them. And if you have no marketable skills, get training in new skills. You don't have to invest in a college degree if that's not your goal.

Chapter 10:

Education And Experience – Your Two Best Friends

Knowledge Arrests Ignorance

This is a summary of what education does. It handcuffs ignorance and puts it in remand until the day of judgment. You cannot unlink yourself from the progress that education has brought.

Most of us grew up knowing that we ought to go to school. The school attendance mindset was ingrained in our young minds. We were told it is the only 'inheritance' that we will ever get from our parents.

Fast forward to today, where is the lie? Education continues to reign supreme. It is almost criminal to be illiterate! Some years ago, education was a luxury. It is now a basic need. This is the metamorphosis of education.

There is, however, another form of education. The kind that does not know about the classroom. It is mostly learned by apprenticeship. It is also a form of education and should not be looked down upon.

Informal education is still practiced to date. It could take the form of rote learning where you have to memorize by repetition and sometimes action a new skill. It neither requires pen nor paper and its results are instantaneous.

One thing with all forms of education is that it has perpetual life. Knowledge is never obsolete. It will forever be useful even if a new skill replaces the old way of doing things.

Experience

Like informal education, experience is not taught in classrooms. It is created from real-life situations that cannot be replayed. When you skip a lesson, you have to wait until life presents a new one.

Experience is the hallmark of the implementation of education. It gives you the chance to put to practice what you have learned. Education prepares you for newer experiences. It is like a teacher training students before they sit for their examination.

The two are never in competition. Instead, they supplement each other. Do not hold onto one and let go of the other. It is their hybrid that will make you sail through in life.

What best friends do.

Education and experience should be your best friends. Having one and lacking the other is like a soldier holding a gun with an empty magazine. It can threaten an enemy but cannot harm them. Of what use is it?

A combination of both provides the following opportunities:

1. A Chance To Serve Your Country

Many patriotic citizens long for the day they will have a chance to serve their mother country in whatever capacity. It is a privilege to have the nation entrust you with its resources.

You can make any call in the best interest of the country. The learned and experienced ones in their fields are best suited for such roles. In dedication, they can improve on any weaknesses and improve the country's strength.

The livelihood of an entire nation cannot be tasked to an inexperienced fellow. Don't you think your country deserves the best?

2. A Mentor To The Upcoming Generation

Mentors are people who are looked upon by others for direction and guidance. They have gone through it all, passed through the fire, tested, and proven to be worthy mentors. This is the value that education and experience bring.

The younger generation deserves the best; someone who will walk them through their experiences in education and in real life. You cannot guide someone through something that you have not experienced.

The value that education and experience add to one's life can be instilled in others. They will emerge stronger and better. An apt student can achieve more than their teacher.

3. A Chance To Eke Out An Honest Livelihood

If you are in it for the money, your two best friends can give it to you on a platter. Education and experience are what every multinational company is looking for. They are searching for people who will add value to their team.

Your newly found best friends are the keys to opening a myriad of opportunities. Your friendship with them will make you exceptional. What more can you ask from lifetime best friends?

Chapter 11:

Choose Getting into Nature for Better Mood and Happiness

It's clear that hiking—and any physical activity—can reduce stress and anxiety. But, there's something about being in nature that may augment those impacts.

In <u>one recent experiment</u> conducted in Japan, participants were assigned to walk either in a forest or in an urban center (taking walks of equal length and difficulty) while having their heart rate variability, heart rate, and blood pressure measured. The participants also filled out questionnaires about their moods, stress levels, and other psychological measures.

Results showed that those who walked in forests had significantly lower heart rates and higher heart rate variability (indicating more relaxation and less stress) and reported better moods and less anxiety than those who walked in urban settings. The researchers concluded that there's something about being in nature that had a beneficial effect on stress reduction, above and beyond what exercise alone might have produced.

In another study, researchers in Finland found that urban dwellers who strolled for as little as 20 minutes through an urban park or woodland reported significantly more stress relief than those who strolled in a city center.

The reasons for this effect are unclear, but scientists believe that we evolved to be more relaxed in natural spaces. In a now-classic laboratory experiment by Roger Ulrich of Texas A&M University and colleagues, participants who first viewed a stress-inducing movie, and were then exposed to color/sound videotapes depicting natural scenes, showed much quicker, more complete recovery from stress than those who'd been exposed to videos of urban settings.

These studies and others provide evidence that being in natural spaces—or even just looking out of a window onto a natural scene—somehow soothes us and relieves stress.

Gregory Bratman of Stanford University has found evidence that nature may impact our mood in other ways, too.

In one 2015 study, he and his colleagues randomly assigned 60 participants to a 50-minute walk in either a natural setting (oak woodlands) or an urban setting (along a four-lane road). Before and after the walk, the participants were assessed on their emotional state and on cognitive measures, such as how well they could perform tasks requiring short-term memory. Results showed that those who walked in nature experienced less anxiety, rumination (focused attention on negative aspects of oneself), and negative affect, as well as more positive emotions, in comparison to the urban walkers. They also improved their performance on the memory tasks.

Chapter 12:

Beginning In A New Stage of Life

A new stage of life can come from an awakening of our self-understanding. We begin to see ourselves differently and clearly. The result is that we may have to make a change in one or more areas of our life.

Another stage is when we experience a significant change in our relationships. Maybe it is marrying for the first time or the birth of your first child. It could even be the change in self-perception that comes following a divorce.

A final example is a stage where we experience a change in jobs or our career direction.

In the first chapter of Circle of Impact: Taking Personal Initiative to Ignite Change, I tell the story of William. He experiences a mid-career transition that requires him to look deeply into his life. He does not have a clear option to remain with the company he served since he graduated from college. He has to decide what this new stage of life will look like.

It is not accidental that new stages of life can be understood from the perspective of the Circle of Impact. For the transition is prompted by one or more of the three dimensions of leadership.

For William, the company (Structure) is changing, and William's family situation (Relationships) requires him to leave the company and begin a new career. William's challenge is understanding what his purpose is, what his skills are, and how both can be marshaled for employment in a new arena.

A new stage of life is less like moving into a new house just like the old house, and more like moving from a cabin in the woods into a high-rise luxury condominium. If we don't treat the change as significant, we find ourselves trying to be a square peg fitting into a round hole.
In effect, we need to step back, pay attention to what is different, listen to what is now expected of us, and allow ourselves the change of mind to fill the role where we will be for the foreseeable future.

Let's take this all too human experience to a deeper level.

You aren't just moving into a new stage of life. This stage requires you to exhibit genuine leadership.

The first step is acknowledging that this new stage will challenge you in new ways.
The next step is to take the three dimensions of leadership and apply them to your new situation. Ask these questions:

1. Are we clear about our purpose? Do we have a clear set of core values that can guide us in our decisions? Are we clear about the expectations for each person's performance?

2. What steps do I need to take to build trust between myself and those whom I'm now leading? Am I clear in my understanding of what each member of the team brings to our work? Do we have the people to cover all aspects of our work together?

3. What kind of structure do we need to maintain a clear focus, good communication, and ensure that we are creating the impact that we desire?

New positions of responsibility require us to also ask these questions.

1. What are my strengths for this new role?

2. What are my limitations? Do we have people on our team whose are strengths are my limitations?

3. Am I prepared to make hard choices? Do I understand what it means for me to operate with integrity?

We all face changes in new stages of life. Some of them project us into areas in which we feel unprepared. If we apply the Circle of Impact model of leadership in each new situation we encounter, we'll find that we come to have a clearer self-understanding and that we are better prepared to make decisions that are necessary.

As you look forward, what do you expect your life to become in the coming years? Anticipating what might come, and actively preparing for that reality will strengthen your self-perception. As a result, a new stage of life that previously would not have been possible now is.

Remember each day to take personal initiative to make a difference that matters, and you'll be prepared for whatever new challenge or opportunity that comes your way.

Chapter 13:

5 Tips to Doing Unique and Meaningful Work

When you think about meaningful work, you think about Mother Theresa or Princess Diana or maybe Peace Corp workers or school teachers and nurses. All of these are great and meaningful jobs. But, not everyone can raise money and attention to help get landmines cleared, nor can (or should) everyone try to teach second grade. And if blood makes you faint, nursing isn't a great idea for you either.

So, how can you make your job meaningful work, even when it's not directly making anyone's life better? These five suggestions will change your job from tedious work to meaningful work.

1. Look at the Big Picture

Why does your job exist? You could be an HR manager, a grocery store cashier, or a tech company CEO. Each of these jobs is necessary to make the world a better place.

Because this is no longer an agrarian society, you need the grocery store cashier to get food. CEOs of well-managed companies provide goods and services to the community and jobs with paychecks for many people. And HR managers can make people's lives much better by helping them progress in their careers, finding and providing the best benefits, and hiring great people.

If you just look at the tasks in front of you, you'll forget how you contribute to the community as a whole.

2. Treat Each Other With Kindness

A kind person can change everyone's day from drudgery to fun. Yes, work is still working, and sometimes it's hard, but working with the right people can make you look forward to working even if the job is hard work.

One man who worked for a brewery as a delivery man could have seen his job as hard work and struggle. After all, his job duty was to drive from restaurant to restaurant, carrying huge kegs of beer and taking out the old, empty ones. But, the people in many restaurants cheered when the beer guy came in with the beer kegs. Their act of kindness changed his job from drudgery to one that he loved.

3. Work Hard

How does working hard make a job meaningful? Well, hard work often equals success. When you succeed in your job, you help others in your department succeed in their jobs. When your whole department succeeds, the company succeeds. That is pretty meaningful.

Additionally, hard work is easier than avoiding work. Think about it: when you have to worry if your boss knows how much time you're spending surfing the internet, that adds another layer of complexity to your job. When you're working hard all of the time, and your boss drops by, it's not a big deal.

When you keep on top of your work, you have lowered stress levels. Now, of course, some people are overburdened and cannot accomplish everything. You might start feeling like, "I can't get everything done, so why bother?" These feelings of stress and failure can pose a huge temptation, but don't give in. First of all, you'll start to feel like your job just isn't meaningful—it's just work. Second, that adds additional stress on top of your head.

What you do instead is go to your boss and say directly, "I have five tasks on my plate right now. I can do four effectively, or I can do a lousy job on all five. Which would you prefer?" or "I have five tasks on my plate right now. I only have time to get three of them done. Which two should I skip?"

4. Look Outside of Your Job

Does your meaningful work have to be your day job? Of course not. Sometimes your day job can fund your meaningful work. Work-life balance means having a life. Whether it's through your family, church, charity, art, or whatever is important to you, you need a paycheck to support that.

You don't have to fulfill all of your needs through your paid job. You don't even need to feel guilty that you're working for a large corporation rather than a small non-profit. It's not bad to earn money. You find your meaning in how you can spend that money.

5. Consider Changing Jobs

If you just can't see how your current job is meaningful, and you can't figure out a way to make your job meaningful work, then perhaps it's time for you to move on. If your job doesn't bring you joy, doesn't allow you to support your family or essential charitable causes, and doesn't help the community, then maybe it's not the right job for you.

No one has a skill set that is so tiny and unique that there is only one job in the world that would suit them. And if you have no marketable skills, get training in new skills. You don't have to invest in a college degree if that's not your goal.

Chapter 14:

Move Towards the Next Thing, Not Away From the Last Thing

I remember when I used to have a bad day, and I remembered the incidents of that day for many days to come. Have you ever had that same thing happen to you? The time when you are trying to remember something important that you want to do today but can't let go of something terrible that happened to you the previous day?

It happens to all of us, and it is reasonable to want to let go of these past experiences or tensions. But do you need to let these things go to work properly on the next big thing?

What if there is another way around this? What if you can work on new projects, activities, and goals and still be at peace with your past? It is possible!

Let's say you have a crucial presentation tomorrow, and you aren't prepared for it mentally. You lack confidence, and you can't shrug off the nervousness. So should you be working more and more on your body language, or should you give up on that presentation altogether and make some excuse?

What if I told you that there was a better way around this problem totally unrelated to it?

Do you have something else that you have adopted as a hobby in your daily routine? May that be a novel, a game, running, gym, cooking, painting, or anything. Just do it! Leave your presentation. Leave it for the morning. Put your notes aside, take a long walk, and indulge fully in your workout sessions. You will see a change in everything, and I say this with experience.

You see, your brain is an immense network of interconnected webs. And we all know that nets get entangled very easily. This is literally the case with our brains as well. When we focus too much on one thing, and there are some tasks pending in our sub-conscience, we try too hard for the first one while trying to forget the latter. This characteristic flaw of human performance and multitasking is something that makes us vulnerable to failure and burnout.

Too much to understand? Let me give it another try!

If you can't do one thing, it's just because your brain needs a deviation. So, give it one! If you can't do it right now, it is because you have run out of ideas to work on it for now. So, leave it for now, start something new, and you will get equipped with some new ideas about the thing you least incomplete previously.

The subtle shift of things will engage new parts of your brain, and it will squeeze out new ideas as soon as you ease the muscle in between your eyes. So don't let go of what you are stuck at right now! Just start something new while re-evaluating your present circumstances. You will get to your desired result one way or another soon.

Chapter 15:

6 Concerning Effects of Mood on Your Life

By definition, mood is the predominant state of our mind which clouds over all the other emotions and judgements. Our mood represents the surface-level condition of our emotional self.

Mood is very versatile and sensitive. Subtle changes in our surroundings or even changes in our thoughts directly affect mood. And consequently, our mood, being the leader of our mental state, affects us, as a whole—even impacting our life directly.

Take notes of these following points so that you can overpower your mood and take complete control of your life.

Here Are 6 Ways How Changes In Your Mood Can Impact Your Life:

6. Mood On Your Judgement and Decision-Making

Humans are the most rational beings—fitted with the most advanced neural organ, the brain. Scientists say that our brain is capable of making one thousand trillion logical operations per second and yet still, we humans are never surprised to make the stupidest of judgements in real life.

Well, along with such an enormous 'Logical reasoning' capacity, our brains also come with an emotional center and that is where mood comes in to crash all logic. Most of the decisions we make are emotional, not logical. Since our emotions are steered by mood, it is no surprise that we often make irrational decisions out of emotional impulses.

But again, there are also some instances where mood-dictated decisions reap better outcomes compared to a logical decision. That's just life.

2. Mood Affects Your Mental Health

While our mood is a holistic reflection of our mental state caused by various external and internal factors, it is also a fact that our mood can be the outcome of some harboring mental illness. Both high degree of euphoria and depression can be an indication of mood disorder—just on two opposite ends of the spectrum.

There is no specific cause behind it except that it is a culmination of prolonged mood irregularities. And mood irregularities may come from anywhere i.e. worrying, quarrelling, drug abuse, period/puberty, hormonal changes etc. If such mood irregularity persists untreated, it may deteriorate your overall mental health and result in more serious conditions. So, consider monitoring your mood changes often.

3. Correlation Between Mood and Physical Well-Being

We have heard the proverb that goes, "A healthy body is a healthy mind". Basically, our body and mind function together. So, if your body is in a healthy state, your mind will reflect it by functioning properly as well. If on the other hand your body is not in a healthy state, due to lack of proper nutrition, sleep, and exercise, then your mind will become weak as well. Yes, according to research, having a persistent bad mood can lead to chronic stress which gradually creates hormonal imbalance in your body and thus, diseases like diabetes, hypertension, stroke etc. may arise in your body. Negative moods can also make you go age faster than usual. So having a cheerful mood not only keeps you happy but also fuels your body and keeps you young. Aim to keep your body in tip top condition to nourish the mind as well.

4. Effect Of Your Mood On Others

This is obvious, right? You wouldn't smile back at your significant other after you have lost your wallet, spilled hot coffee all over yourself and missed the only bus to your job interview.

Your mood overshadows how you behave with others. The only way to break out of this would be to meditate and achieve control over your emotional volatility—believe that whatever happened, happened for a reason. Your sully mood doesn't warrant being hostile with others. Instead, talk to people who want the best of you. Express your griefs.

5. Mood As A Catalyst In Your Productivity

Tech giants like Google, Apple, Microsoft all have certain 'play areas' for the employees to go and play different games. It is there to remove mental stress of the employees because mood is an essential factor in determining your productivity at work-place. According to experts, people with a negative mood are 10% less productive in their work than those who are in a positive mood. This correlation between mood and productivity is an important thing to be concerned about.

6. Mood Change Your Perspective

Everyone has their own point of view. Perspectives of people vary from individual to individual and similarly, it varies depending on the mood of an individual. On a bad day, even your favorite Starbucks drink would feel tasteless. It doesn't mean that they made a bad drink—it means that you're not in the mood of enjoying its taste. So, how you perceive things and people is greatly affected by your mindset. Pro-tip: Don't throw judgement over someone or something carrying a bad mood. You'll regret it later and think "I totally misread this".

Final Thoughts

Our mood has plenty of implications on our life. Though our mood is an external representation of our overall mental state, it has its effect on very miniscule aspects of our life to large and macroscopic levels. In the long run, our mood alone can be held responsible for what we have done our whole life—the choices we've made. Though it is really difficult to control our mood, we can always try. Meditating may be one of the possible ways to have our mood on the noose. Because no matter what happens, you wouldn't want your whole life to be an outcome of your emotional impulses would you?

Chapter 16:

Six Habits of Self-Love

We can show gratitude to ourselves for our different achievements in many ways. It is something that most people overlook as a waste of time and resources. This is a fallacy. It is high time we develop habits of self-love, to recharge our bodies and minds in preparation for another phase of achievements.

Here are six habits of self-love:

1. Treating Yourself

It is showing gratitude to yourself by way of satisfying your deepest desires instead of waiting for someone else to do it for you. Take the personal initiative to go shopping and buy that designer suit or dress you have been wanting so badly. Do not wait for someone else to do it for you while you are capable.

Take that much-needed vacation and a break from work to be with your family. Spend time with the people you love and cherish every moment because, in this fast-moving world, the future is uncertain. Secure your happiness lest you drown in depression. The best person to take care of your interests is yourself.

Who will take you out for swimming or outing to those posh hotels if you do not initiate it? Self-love begins when you realize your worth and do not allow anyone else to bring it down.

2. Celebrate Your Victories

Take advantage of every opportunity to celebrate your wins, no matter how small. A habit of self-love is to celebrate your achievements and ignore voices that discourage you. Nothing should muffle you from shouting your victories to the world. The testimony of your victory will encourage a stranger not to give up in his/her quest.

It is neither pride nor boastfulness. It is congratulating yourself for the wins that you rightfully deserve. How else can you love yourself if you do not appreciate yourself for the milestones you have conquered? Do not shy away from thanking yourself, privately or publicly, because no one else best knows your struggles except yourself.

3. Accept Yourself

To begin with, accept your social and economic status because you know the battles you have fought. Self-acceptance is an underrated form of self-love. Love yourself and accept your shortcomings. When you learn to accept yourself, other people will in turn accept you. They will learn how to accommodate you in the same manner you learned to live with all your imperfections.

Self-loathing dies when you master self-acceptance and self-love. Self-care keeps off self-rejection. You begin seeing your worth and great potential. It is the enemy within that is responsible for the fall of great empires.

The enemy within is low self-esteem and self-rejection. Accept the things you cannot change and change the things in your ability. Do not be hard on yourself because a journey of a thousand miles begins with a single step.

4. Practice Forgiveness

Forgiveness is a strong act. When you forgive those who wrong you, you let go of unnecessary baggage. It is unhealthy to live with a heart full of hate (pun intended). Forgiveness does not mean that you have allowed other people to wrong you repetitively. It means you have outgrown their wrong acts and you no longer allow their inconsiderate acts to affect you. Forgiveness benefits the forgiver more than the forgiven. It heals the heart from any hurt caused. It is the best form of self-care yet difficult at the same time. Forgiveness is a gradual process initiated by the bigger person in any conflict. Practicing self-care is by recognizing the importance of turning a new leaf and staying free from shackles of grudges and bitterness.

Unforgiveness builds bitterness and vengeance. It finally clouds your judgment and you become irrational. Choosing forgiveness is a vote on self-care.

5. Choose Your Associates Wisely

Associate with progressive people. Show me your friends and I will tell you the kind of person you are. Your friends have the potential to either build or destroy your appreciation of self-worth. They will trim your excesses and supplement your deficiencies. A cadre of professionals tends to share several traits.
Self-care involves taking care of your mental state and being selective of who you let into your personal space. It supersedes all other interests.

6. Engaging In Hobbies

Hobbies are the activities we do during our free time to relax our minds and bond with our friends. When doing these hobbies we are at ease and free from pressures of whatever form. We need to take a break from our daily work routine from time to time and do other social activities.

Hobbies are essential to explore other interests and rejuvenate our psyche and morale. Self-love places your interests and well-being above everything else. There is a thin line between it and selfishness, but it is not the latter.

These six habits of self-love will ensure you have peace and sobriety of mind to make progressive decisions.

Chapter 17:

6 Steps To Focus on Growth

Growth is a lifelong process. We grow every moment from the day we are born until our eventual death. And the amazing thing about growth is that there is no real limit to it.

Now, what exactly is growth? Well, growing is the process of changing from one state to another and usually, it has to be positive; constructive; better-than-before. Although growth occurs equally towards all directions in the early years of our life, the rate of growth becomes more and more narrowed down to only a few particular aspects of our life as we become old. We become more distinctified as individuals, and due to our individuality, not everyone of us can possibly grow in all directions. With our individual personality, experiences, characteristics, our areas of growth become unique to us. Consequently, our chances of becoming successful in life corresponds to how we identify our areas of growth and beam them on to our activities with precision. Let us explore some ways to identify our key areas of growth and utilize them for the better of our life.

1. Identify Where You Can Grow

For a human being, growth is relative. One person cannot grow in every possible way because that's how humans are—we simply cannot do every thing at once. One person may grow in one way while another may grow in a completely different way. Areas of growth can be so unlike that one's positive growth might even seem like negative growth to another person's perspective. So, it is essential that we identify the prime areas where we need to grow. This can be done through taking surveys, asking people or critically analyzing oneself. Find out what lackings do you have as a human being, find out what others think that you lack as a human being. Do different things and note down where you are weak but you have to do it anyway. Then, make a list of those areas where you need growing and move on to the next step.

2. Accept That You Need To Grow In Certain Areas

After carefully identifying your lackings, accept these in your conscious and subconscious mind. Repeatedly admit to yourself and others that you lack so and so qualities where you wish to grow with time.

Never feel ashamed of your shortcomings. Embrace them comfortably because you cannot truly change yourself without accepting that you need to change. Growth is a dynamic change that drags you way out of your comfort zone and pushes you into the wild. And to start on this endeavor for growth, you need to have courage. Growth is a choice that requires acceptance and humility.

3. Remind Yourself of Your Shortcomings

You can either write it down and stick it on your fridge or just talk about it in front of people you've just met—this way, you'll constantly keep reminding yourself that you have to grow out of your lackings. And this remembrance will tell you to try—try improving little by little. Try growing.

It is important to remain consciously aware of these at all times because you never know when you might have to face what. All the little and big things you encounter every day are all opportunities of growth. This takes us to the fourth step:

4. Face Your Problems

Whatever you encounter, in any moment or place in your life is an opportunity created: an opportunity for learning. A very old adage goes: "the more we learn, the more we grow". So, if you don't face your problems and run away from them, then you are just losing the opportunity to learn from it, and thus, losing the opportunity of growing from it. Therefore, facing whatever life throws at you also has an important implication on your overall growth. Try to make yourself useful against all odds. Even if you fail at it, you will grow anyway.

5. Cross The Boundary

So, by now you have successfully identified your areas of growth, you have accepted them, you constantly try to remind yourself of them and you face everything that comes up, head on—never running away. You are already making progress. Now comes the step where you push yourself beyond your current status. You go out of what you are already facing and make yourself appear before even more unsettling circumstances.

This is a very difficult process, but if you grow out of here, nothing can stop you ever. And only a few people successfully make it through. You create your own problems, no one might support you and yet still, you try to push forward, make yourself overcome new heights of difficulties and grow like the tallest tree in the forest. You stand out of the crowd. This can only be done in one or two subjects in a lifetime. So make sure that you know where you want to grow. Where you want to invest that much effort, and time, and dedication. Then, give everything to it. Growth is a life's journey.

6. Embrace Your Growth

After you have crossed the boundary, there is no turning back. You have achieved new heights in your life, beyond what you thought you could have ever done. The area—the subject in which you tried to develop yourself, you have made yourself uniquely specialized in that particular area. You have outgrown the others in that field. It is time for you to make yourself habituated with that and embrace it gracefully. The wisdom you've accumulated through growth is invaluable—it has its roots deeply penetrated into your life. The journey that you've gone through while pursuing your growth will now define you. It is who you are.

As I've mentioned in the first line, "growth is a lifelong process". Growth is not a walk in the park, It is you tracking through rough terrains—steep heights and unexplored depths for an entire lifetime. Follow these simple yet difficult steps; grow into the tallest tree and your life will shine upon you like the graceful summer sun.

Chapter 18:

6 Steps To Get Out of Your Comfort Zone

The year 2020 and 2021 have made a drastic change in all our lives, which might have its effect forever. The conditions of last year and a half have made a certain lifestyle choice for everyone, without having a say in it for us.

This new lifestyle has been a bit overwhelming for some and some started feeling lucky. Most of us feel comfortable working from home, and taking online classes while others want to have some access to public places like parks and restaurants.

But the pandemic has affected everyone more than once. And now we are all getting used to this relatively new experience of doing everything from home. Getting up every day to the same routine and the same environment sometimes takes us way back on our physical and mental development and creativity.

So, one must learn to leave the comfort zone and keep themselves proactive. Here are some ways anyone can become more productive and efficient.

Everyone is always getting ready to change but never changing.

1. Remember your Teenage Self

People often feel nostalgic remembering those days of carelessness when they were kids and so oblivious in that teenage. But, little do they take for inspiration or motivation from those times. When you feel down, or when you don't feel like having the energy for something, just consider your teenage self at that time.

If only you were a teenager now, you won't be feeling lethargic or less motivated. Rather you'd be pushing harder and harder every second to get the job done as quickly as possible. If you could do it back then, you still can! All you need is some perspective and a medium to compare to.

2. Delegate or Mentor someone

Have you ever needed to have someone who could provide you some guidance or help with a problem that you have had for some time?

I'm sure, you weren't always a self-made man or a woman. Somewhere along the way, there was someone who gave you the golden quote that changed you consciously or subconsciously.

Now is the time for you to do the same for someone else. You could be a teacher, a speaker, or even a mentor who doesn't have any favors to ask in return. Once you get the real taste of soothing someone else's pain, you won't hesitate the next time.

This feeling of righteousness creates a chain reaction that always pushes you to get up and do good for anyone who could need you.

3. Volunteer in groups

The work of volunteering may seem pointless or philanthropic. But the purpose for you to do it should be the respect that you might get, but the stride to get up on your feet and help others to be better off.

Volunteering for flood victims, earthquake affectees or the starving people of deserts and alpines can help you understand the better purpose of your existence. This keeps the engine of life running.

4. Try New Things for a Change

Remember the time in Pre-school when your teachers got you to try drawing, singing, acting, sculpting, sketching, and costume parties. Those weren't some childish approach to keep you engaged, but a planned system to get your real talents and skills to come out.

We are never too old to learn something new. Our passions are unlimited just as our dreams are. We only need a push to keep discovering the new horizons of our creative selves.

New things lead to new people who lead to new places which might lead to new possibilities. This is the circle of life and life is ironic enough to rarely repeat the same thing again.

You never know which stone might lead you to a gold mine. So never stop discovering and experiencing because this is what makes us the supreme being.

5. Push Your Physical Limits

This may sound cliched, but it always is the most important point of them all. You can never get out of your comfort zone, till you see the world through the hard glass.

The world is always softer on one side, but the image on the other side is far from reality. You can't expect to get paid equally to the person who works 12 hours a day in a large office of hundreds of employees. Only if you have the luxury of being the boss of the office.

You must push yourself to search for opportunities at every corner. Life has always more and better to offer at each stop, you just have to choose a stop.

6. Face Your Fears Once and For All

People seem to have a list of Dos and Dont's. The latter part is mostly because of a fear or a vacant thought that it might lead to failure for several reasons.

You need a "Do it all" behavior in life to have an optimistic approach to everything that comes in your way.

What is the biggest most horrible thing that can happen if you do any one of these things on your list? You need to have a clear vision of the possible worst outcome.

If you have a clear image of what you might lose, now must try to go for that thing and remove your fear once and for all. Unless you have something as important as your life to lose, you have nothing to fear from anything.

No one can force you to directly go skydiving if you are scared of heights. But you can start with baby steps, and then, maybe, later on in life you dare to take a leap of faith.

"Life is a rainbow, you might like one color and hate the other. But that doesn't make it ugly, only less tempting".

All you need is to be patient and content with what you have today, here, right now. But you should never stop aiming for more. And you certainly shouldn't regret it if you can't have or don't have it now.

People try to find their week spots and frown upon those moments of hard luck. What they don't realize is, that the time they wasted crying for what is in the past, could have been well spent for a far better future they could cherish for generations to come.

Chapter 19:

6 Ways On How To Change Your Body Language To Attract Success

"If you want to find the truth, do not listen to the words coming to you. Rather see the body language of the speaker. It speaks the facts not audible." - Bhavesh Chhatbar.

Our body language is exceptionally essential as 60-90% of our communication with others is nonverbal. If properly used, it can be our key to more tremendous success. We focus more on our business plans, our marketing drives, and our spreadsheets rather than considering our facial expressions, posture, or what our physical gestures might be saying about us. Our mindset also plays a role in how our body language expresses itself. No matter how impressive our words maybe, if we are sending a negative signal with our body language, we would eventually lose the opportunities of gaining more success.

Here is a list to help you change your body language to attract more success.

1. The Power of Voice

Your personal voice has a huge impact and can literally make or break your success. It is one of the most direct routes to empower your communication. The pitch of your voice, its timbre, cadence, volume, and the speed with which you speak, are all influential factors that will ensure how convincing you are and how people will judge your character. Lowering your voice at the right moment or injecting some spontaneity into it when needed will enhance your credibility and lend you an air of intelligence. We must fill our voices with our range and depth if we want others and ourselves to take us seriously.

2. The Power of Listening

An excellent speaking skill represents only half of the leadership expression. The other half is mastering your art in listening. While a good listener is incredibly rare, it is essential to keep our ears open to any valuable information that is often silently transmitted. When we start listening attentively to others, we begin to notice what a person is saying and decode accurately what they don't say. You will also begin to realize what the other person is thinking or whether their attitude is positive or hostile towards you. With these particular observations, you will likely attune to another person and create the bond crucial to a successful working life.

3. The Necessity for Emotional Intelligence

The skill of acute listening develops our emotional intelligence, the intuition to ascertain the objective reality of the situation. When we lack emotional intelligence, we might misinterpret situations and fail to decipher what might be needed. Emotional intelligence deepens our empathy. It gives us the ability to be present and listen to someone when they need it the most. It is the single best predictor of performance in the workplace and can be the most vital driver of personal excellence and leadership. Our understanding of emotional intelligence will vastly improve our internal relations and can also deepen our sense of personal fulfillment and professional accomplishment.

4. The Power of Eye Contact

Making eye contact and holding it is seen as a sign of confidence, and the other person is felt valued. It increases your chance of being trustful and respected as they tend to listen to you more attentively and feel comfortable giving you their insights. You may be shy, an introvert, or might have heard that it's impolite to maintain eye contact with a superior. But in many parts of the world, business people expect you to maintain eye contact 50-60% of the time. Here's a simple tip: when you meet someone, look into their eyes long enough to notice their eye color.

5. Talk With Your Hands

There's a region in our brain called the Broca's area, which is essential and active during our speech production and when we wave our hands. Gestures are integrally linked to speech, so gesturing while talking can speed up your thinking. Using hand gestures while talking can improve verbal content as well as make your speechless hesitant. You will see that it will help you form clearer thoughts with more declarative language and speak in tighter sentences.

6. Strike A Power Pose

Research conducted at Harvard and Columbia Business Schools into the effects of body posture and confidence show that holding your body in expansive high-power poses (such as leaning back with hands behind the head or standing with legs and arms stretched wide open) for only as little as two minutes can stimulate high levels of testosterone (a hormone linked to power) and lower levels of cortisol (a stress hormone). You will look and feel more confident and inevitable, leading to an increased feeling of energy and a high tolerance for risk.

Conclusion

Most of our body language and movement are subconscious, so it can be challenging to retrain ourselves away from habits we have had for years. Still, we must try to master our body language, too, with the art of public speaking. Regular practice Is the key to success and the quickest route to attain confident body language as with any other skill. Practice them in your day-to-day life so that they may become deep-rooted. Be less compliant and step into an edgier, emboldened, and more genuine you.

Chapter 20:

6 Ways To Adopt A Better Lifestyle For Long-Term Success

A good lifestyle leads to a good life. The important choices we make throughout our lives impact our future in numerous ways. The need to make ourselves better in every aspect of life and the primary ability to perform such a routine can be a lifestyle. There is no proper way to live written in a book; however, through our shared knowledge and our comprehension, we can shape a lifestyle that can be beneficial and exciting at the same time. Though there is no doubt that falling into a specific routine can be difficult but, maintaining a proper state is more critical for a successful life.

For long-term success, a good lifestyle is a priority. Almost everything we do in our lives directly or indirectly involves our future self. So, a man needs to become habitual of such things that can profit him in every way possible. To visualize a better you, You need to configure just about everything around you. And to change all the habits that may make you feel lagging. The most common feature of a better lifestyle for long-term success is determination.

1. Change in Pattern Of Your Life

It is good to shape a pattern of living from the start and forming good habits, engaging yourself in profitable practice, and choosing a healthier custom. It feels impossible to change something you have already been habitual of, but willpower is the key. With some motivation and dedication, you can change yourself into a better version of yourself. You are choosing what might be suitable for you and staying determined on that thought. The first step is to let go of harmful things slowly because letting go of habits and patterns that you are used to can be challenging. After some, sometimes you will notice yourself letting go of things more easily.

2. Take Your Time

Time is an essential factor when it comes to forming a lifestyle for a successful life. Time can seem to slow through the process, making us think that it may have been stopped in our most difficult moments. Similarly, making us feel it goes flying by when our life is relaxed and at ease. Time never stops for anyone. It is crucial to make sure we make most of our time and consume it in gaining more knowledge and power. Take time to inform your lifestyle, but not more than required. We are taking things at a moderate pace so you can both enjoy life and do work.

3. Don't Always Expect Things To Go Your Way

As much as we humans like to get our hopes high, we can't always expect things to go our way. Even things we have worked hard for can sometimes go downhill. It is at times overconfidence, but sometimes it can be pure bad luck. We can't get disheartened by something that was not meant to go a specific way. Don't expect perfection in all the work you do. Staying patient is the walk towards the reward. And making the best out of the worst can be the only way to get yourself going.

4. Don't Be Afraid To Ask For Help

It is human nature to ask each other for help now and then. If it comes to this point, don't be afraid to ask for help yourself. Ask someone superior to aid you on matters you find difficult. Don't hesitate to ask your inferiors who might have more knowledge than you in some certain customs. Help them, too, if needed. Ask them to assist you out on points, but never make them do the whole project. Don't make someone do something you wouldn't do yourself.

5. Be Prompt In Everything

Lagging behind your work can be the worst possible habit you could raise. Make yourself punctual in every aspect. Make sure you are on time everywhere. Either it's to wake up in the morning or to go to a meeting. Laziness can never be proven good for you or your dream towards a prosperous lifestyle. Respect time, and it shall respect you. Show your colleges that they can depend on you to show up on time and take responsibility for work. You would rather wait than making others wait for you. That will show you seriousness toward your business.

6. Keep A Positive Attitude

Keeping a positive attitude can lead to a positive lifestyle. Be happy with yourself in every context, and make sure that everything you do has your complete confidence. Be thankful to all who surround you. Keep a positive attitude, whether it be a home or office. Speak with your superiors with respect and make yourself approachable around inferiors. Your positive mindset can affect others in a way too. They will become more inclined towards you, and they can easily suggest you help someone.

Conclusion

Just about everything in your life affects your future in a way or other, so make sure that you do all you can to make yourself worth the praise. Keep your lifestyle simple but effective. Try to do as much as possible for yourself and make time to relax as well. For long-term success, willpower is the most important; make sure you have it. Keep your headlight and calm for the upcoming difficulties and prepare yourself to face almost everything life throws at you.

Chapter 21:

6 Ways To Transform Your Thinking

Changing your mindset isn't easy, but an open and positive attitude. Personal growth contributes to our choices to achieve physical, emotional, and spiritual well-being. Even something as simple as changing your mind can change your life. It's essential to take time for your mindset. During this period, we begin to understand ourselves, making us more compassionate and patient with ourselves. Our societies and cultures thrive in the professions that life brings to our lives and our tables. In this regard, the use of "bandage" solutions and rapid remedies to overcome certain obstacles in our lives have implications. These decisions never last long and are a matter of time and effort to slow down, ground up, and shift focus. Changing your mind means becoming more optimistic and giving your mind the breathing space it needs to grow and expand. It's about looking at everything that doesn't work for you and being open to other methods that might help.

1. Practice Mindfulness

To adopt a more positive mindset, you must first recognize your current mindset. As you develop mindfulness, you can recognize and identify habituated thought patterns and then decide whether to use them or not. Mindfulness creates a distance between you and your thoughts, allowing you to see yourself separate from them. Incorporate mindfulness into your morning or evening routine and sit quietly for a few minutes (and practice gradually increasing the amount of time). When a thought comes to mind, turn your attention to your breathing instead of clinging to it.

2. Address Your Inner Critic

Your inner critic likes to convince you that it's not true, which often makes you feel pretty bad. Think of this voice as separate from you. Challenge the lie he is trying to feed you. Ask yourself. Is it true? Is there any evidence to support this claim? Another way is to thank this inner voice for their opinion and then say "no." I prefer not to fall into these negative thoughts. Alternatively, you may choose shorter, more direct answers, such as Not Now or Delete.

3. Know Your Trigger

It is essential to be aware of certain people, situations, and situations to trigger more negative thoughts. Meeting your boss or making important life decisions can make you overly critical of yourself or question your worth. Once you become aware of your triggers, you can better prepare to control your thoughts than go back to your old negative thinking patterns. It is also helpful to see which cognitive biases, such as those mentioned above, recur most often.

4. Write It Out

Writing down your feelings on paper is a great way to relieve your thoughts and learn more about them. We often don't realize how harmful our thoughts are. Negative thinking patterns become habitual over time and usually go unnoticed. Taking notes makes it easier to identify areas that need attention. You can also ask questions as soon as they appear in the article to ensure they are accurate and relevant. If not, let them go or replace them with more positive thoughts. Writing in a diary, the first thing you do when you wake up in the morning is the perfect time to write down your stream of consciousness on paper.

5. Recite A Mantra

Shouting out a mantra or positive affirmation is a great way to break free from your current negative thoughts. When you feel that something negative is coming, you can make it a habit to recite or focus on it several times throughout the day. You can choose words or phrases that remind you to focus on the present and focus more on the positive.

6. Change Your Surroundings

Sometimes the thoughts are so loud that it is best to change the physical environment. Go for a walk, run or meet friends in nature. The point is to engage in something other than a negative cycle so you can get back to the problem when you're in a cleaner space. Choose your favourite activity or place, and you will feel better. If you need to be with others, have people around you to encourage you to think positively. (Avoid the trigger!)

Negative stereotypes of thoughts are challenging to break, especially when habituated. Patterns that have existed for years don't disappear overnight, so it's essential to show compassion and patience for yourself as you work.

Chapter 22:

8 Habits That Can Make You Happy

We're always striving for something, whether it's a promotion, a new truck, or anything else. This brings us to an assumption that "when this happens, You'll finally be happy."

While these important events ultimately make us happy, research suggests that this pleasure does not last. A Northwestern University study compared the happiness levels of ordinary people to those who had won the massive lottery in the previous years. It was found that the happiness scores of both groups were nearly equal.

The false belief that significant life events determine your happiness or sorrow is so widespread that psychologists have given it a name- "impact bias." The truth is that event-based happiness is transitory. Satisfaction is artificial; either create it or not. Long-term happiness is achieved through several habits. Happy people develop behaviors that keep them satisfied daily.

Here are eight habits that can make you happy.

1. Take Pride in Life's Little Pleasures

We are prone to falling into routines by nature. This is, in some ways, a positive thing. It helps conserve brainpower while also providing comfort. However, it is possible to be so engrossed in your routine that you neglect to enjoy the little pleasures in life. Happy people understand the value of savoring the taste of their meal, revel in a great discussion they just had, or even simply stepping outside to take a big breath of fresh air.

2. Make Efforts To Be Happy

Nobody, not even the most ecstatically happy people, wakes up every day feeling this way. They work harder than everyone else. They understand how easy it is to fall into a routine where you don't check your emotions or actively strive to be happy and optimistic. People who are happy continually assess their moods and make decisions with their happiness in mind.

3. Help Other People

Helping others not only makes them happy, but it also makes you happy. Helping others creates a surge of dopamine, oxytocin, and serotonin, all of which generate pleasant sensations. According to Harvard research, people who assist others are ten times more likely to be focused at work and 40% more likely to be promoted. According to the same study, individuals who constantly provide social support are the most likely to be happy during stressful situations. As long as you don't overcommit yourself, helping others will positively affect your mood.

4. Have Deep Conversations.

Happy people understand that happiness and substance go hand in hand. They avoid gossip, trivial conversation, and passing judgment on others. Instead, they emphasize meaningful interactions. You should interact with others on a deeper level because it makes you feel good, creates emotional connections, and, importantly, it's an intriguing way to learn.

5. Get Enough Sleep

I've pounded this one too hard over the years, and I can't emphasize enough how important sleep is for enhancing your attitude, focus, and self-control. When you sleep, your brain recharges, removing harmful proteins that accumulate as byproducts of regular neuronal activity during the day. This guarantees that you awaken alert and focused. When you don't get enough quality sleep, your energy, attention, and memory all suffer. Even in the absence of a stressor, sleep loss elevates stress hormone levels. Sleep is vital to happy individuals because it makes them feel good, and they know how bad they feel when they don't get enough sleep.

6. Surround Yourself With the Right People

Happiness is contagious; it spreads through people. Surrounding yourself with happy people boosts your confidence, encourages your creativity, and is simply enjoyable. Spending time with negative people has the opposite effect. They get others to join their self-pity party so that they may feel better about themselves. Consider this: if someone was smoking, would you sit there all afternoon inhaling the second-hand smoke? You'd step back, and you should do the same with negative people.

7. Always Stay Positive

Everyone, even happy people, encounters difficulties daily. Instead of moaning about how things could or should have been, happy people think about what they are grateful for. Then they find the best approach to the situation, that is, dealing with it and moving on. Pessimism is a powerful source of sadness. Aside from the damaging effects on your mood, the problem with a pessimistic mindset is that it becomes a self-fulfilling prophecy. If you expect bad things, you are more likely to encounter horrific events. Gloomy thoughts are difficult to overcome unless you see how illogical they are. If you force yourself to look at the facts, you'll discover that things aren't nearly as awful as you think.

8. Maintain a Growth Mindset

People's core attitudes can be classified into two types: fixed mindsets and growth mindsets. You believe you are who you are and cannot change if you have a fixed attitude. When you are challenged, this causes problems because anything that looks to be more than you can handle will make you feel despondent and overwhelmed. People with a growth mindset believe that with effort, they can progress. They are happy as a result of their improved ability to deal with adversity. They also outperform those with a fixed perspective because they welcome difficulties and see them as chances to learn something new.

Conclusion

It can be tough to maintain happiness but investing your energy in good habits will pay off. Adopting even a couple of the habits on this list will have a significant impact on your mood.

Chapter 23:

How To Trick Yourself Into Doing Anything

You have a life full of passion that you yet do not possess. You have a life where you are content with what you have, and you are more than happy to settle for less. You have this feeling in your gut that stops you from pushing because you are afraid to lose it all. So you feel blessed with whatever you get your hands on.

Close your eyes and look into your future twenty years from now. Look if you find yourself in a house with everything you have ever dreamed about. Don't push what you think in that image; instead, see what you wish to have. If you can't find it and if you feel a grain of doubt, this is where you are going to end up. If you keep beating around the bushes, this is your dark, uncertain future.

Yes, we all get it. You have a grind in your life that you can't avoid. We all have! But not all of us are the same twenty years from now. You can tell yourself all the lies and be pleased with whatever you have on your plate. But why have a small plate when you have a bigger appetite?

You are ready to settle for less because you are not ready to believe. You are not ready to believe that you can do it. You are not ready to believe that things can happen to you. You are uncertain about the fact that you, too, can have the wealth that others wish to get. But you are too shabby to be able to get to that place of certainty.

If you want things to happen for you, punch this on your mind; you and only you have to believe in yourself before anyone else to be able to do anything. You are playing with a part of your body that is trying to go above a cohesive system that is yourself. You only need to trick that part of your body, and then you will have everything you wish to have.

So go play with that part, make bets with it and think of it as the one thing you want to beat before anything else. You know what I am talking about, right? It's your own mind! Your mind is the one thing that needs to be beaten that will make you the invincible being you have always wanted to be.

How many failed marriages have you had? How many failed businesses have you had? How many failed semesters have you had? How many failed jobs have you had? All these things make you feel worthless, and you can't push yourself not to do these things again. I am not saying that you do all this by choice but avoiding all this isn't your choice either. Because if it was, there is no chance you can't put that thing in your head to good use.

You are in the same rut you were in ten years ago. But if you change even a single thing now, everything from there will change a different path altogether.

Chapter 24:

Being Authentic

Today we're going to talk about the topic of authenticity. This topic is important because for many of us, we are told to put on a poker face and to act in ways that are politically correct. We are told by our parents, Teachers, and many other figures of authority to try to change who we are to fit society's norms and standards. Over time this constant act of being told to be different can end up forcing us to be someone who we are not entirely.

We start to behave in ways that are not true to ourselves. We start to act and say things that might start to appear rehearsed and fake, and we might not even notice this change until we hear whispers from colleagues or friends of friends that tell us we appear to be a little fake. On some level it isn't our fault as well, or it might be. Whatever the reason is, what we can do however is to make the effort to be more authentic.

So why do we need to be authentic? Well technically there's no one real reason that clearly defines why this is important. It actually depends on what we want to expect from others and in life in general. If we want to develop close bonds and friendships, it requires us to be honest and to be real. Our friends can tell very easily when it seems we are trying to hide something or if we are not being genuine or deceptive in the things we say. If people manage to detect that we are insincerity, they might easily choose to not be our friend or may start to distance themselves from us. If we are okay with that, then i guess being authentic is not a priority in this area.

When we choose to be authentic, we are telling the world that we are not afraid to speak our mind, that we are not afraid to be vocal of our opinions and not put on a mask to try and hide and filter how we present ourselves. Being authentic also helps people trust you more easily. When you are real with others, they tend to be real with you too. And this helps move the partnership along more quickly. Of course if this could also be a quick way to get into conflicts if one doesn't practice abit of caution in the things that they say that might be hurtful.

Being authentic builds your reputation as someone who is relatable. As humans we respond incredibly well to people who come across as genuine, kind, and always ready to help you in times of need. The more you open up to someone, they can connect with you on a much deeper emotional connection.

If you find yourself struggling with building lasting friendships, stop trying to be someone who you are not. You are not Kim Kardashian, Justin Bieber, or someone else. You are you, and you are beautiful. If there are areas of yourself you feel are lacking, work on it. But make sure you never try to hide the real you from others. You will find that life is much easier when you stop putting on a mask and just embracing and being you are meant to be all along.

Chapter 25:

Confidence: The Art of Humble-Pride

There is a very fine line between confidence and overconfidence, being bold and being belligerent, having authority and having arrogance. It is a line that trips even the most nimble footed, but usually because they have dedicated no clear thoughts on how to manage it. Instead, they follow their gut on how far they can push or how much they should hold back.

This is the paradox; you need to be confident. You need self-belief, you need to be assured of your ability and sometimes even certain of what the outcome will be. All of those things are empowering. In the words of Tony Robbins, you have to awaken the giant within. But had Goliath stooped to consider David's sling he would have worn a different helmet. The problem was that Goliath had a belief that he was fully capable of everything just as he was. I like to call it confidence without context, or universal, unanimous support of the self. That is the dangerous kind of confidence that spills over into arrogance. Chess grandmasters will tell you that the moment you assume you will win is the moment you lose. Because that is precisely when you start to make mistakes. You become too focussed on what your next move is that you don't even see theirs. You become so absorbed in your strategy that you fail to account for their plan and the bigger picture. It was confidence without context that made Goliath run straight towards to the flying stone.

Confidence without context is an assumption. And the problem with assumptions is that they go one step beyond the rationality of an expectation. Assumption goes into the fight drunk, having already celebrated the victory. But that leads to its inevitable demise. Expectation remains present, it acknowledges the reality of the situation. Assumption arrives intoxicated, expectation arrives in control. That is the difference.

Pride is the greatest antidote to reason, which makes humility its greatest ally. If you want to stay in the fight you need to have both confidence and humility. If you want to stay competitive, if you want to get a promotion, if you want to level up. Whatever it is that you want, I can guarantee that the path to get there is a hopscotch of humility and confidence. Every bold step forward must be followed by a humble one. Note that humility does not take you backwards, it keeps you balanced.

You can hop along in arrogance, but you will never last as long or be as strong as the one who keeps an even stride. If you strive for something, then you need to start striding towards it. And the rhythm of your march should beat to the sounds of a two-tone drum. Because confidence without context is like hopping upstairs – you might reach the second floor, but you will never manage the pyramid.

Chapter 26:

Deal With Your Fears Now

Fear is a strange thing.

Most of our fears are phantoms that never actually appear or become real,

Yet it holds such power over us that it stops us from making steps forward in our lives.

It is important to deal with fear as it not only holds you back but also keeps you caged in irrational limitations.

Your life is formed by what you think.

It is important not to dwell or worry about anything negative.

Don't sweat the small stuff, and it's all small stuff (Richard Carlson).

It's a good attitude to have when avoiding fear.

Fear can be used as a motivator for yourself.

If you're in your 30s, you will be in your 80s in 50 years, then it will be too late.

And that doesn't mean you will even have 50 years. Anything could happen.

But let's say you do, that's 50 years to make it and enjoy it.

But to enjoy it while you are still likely to be healthy, you have a maximum of 15 years to make it - minus sleep and living you are down to 3 years. If, however you are in your 40s, you better get a move on quickly.

Does that fear not dwarf any possible fears you may have about taking action now?
Dealing with other fears becomes easy when the ticking clock is staring you in the face.
Most other fears are often irrational.

We are only born with two fears, the fear of falling and the fear of load noises.
The rest have been forced on us by environment or made up in our own minds.
The biggest percentage of fear never actually happens.

To overcome fear, we must stare it in the face and walk through it knowing our success is at the other side.
Fear is a dream killer and often stops people from even trying.
Whenever you feel fear and think of quitting, imagine behind you is the ultimate fear of the clock ticking away your life.

If you stop, you lose, and the clock is a bigger monster than any fear.
If you let anything stop, you the clock will catch you.

So, stop letting these small phantoms prevent you from living,
They are stealing your seconds, minutes, hours, days and weeks.

If you carry on being scared, they will take your months, years and decades.
Before you know it, they have stolen your life.

You are stronger than fear, but you must display true strength that fear will be scared.
It will retreat from your path forever if you move in force towards it because fear is fear and by definition is scared.

We as humans are the scariest monsters on planet Earth.
So we should have nothing to fear
Fear tries to stop us from doing our life's work and that is unacceptable.
We must view life's fears as the imposters they are, mere illusions in our mind trying to control us.

We are in control here.
We have the free will to do it anyway despite fear.
Take control and fear will wither and disappear as if it was never here.
The control was always yours you just let fear steer you off your path.

Fear of failure, fear of success, fear of what people will think.
All irrational illusions.
All that matters is what you believe.
If your belief and faith in yourself is strong, fear will be no match for your will.

Les Brown describes fear as false evidence appearing real.

I've never seen a description so accurate.

Whenever fear rears its ugly head, just say to yourself this is false evidence appearing real.

Overcoming fear takes courage and strength in oneself.

We must develop more persistence than the resistance we will face when pursuing our dreams.

If we do not develop a thick skin and unwavering persistence we will be beaten by fear, loss and pain.

Our why must be so important that these imposters become small in comparison.

Because after all the life we want to live does dwarf any fears or set back that might be on the path.

Fear is insignificant.

Fear is just one thing of many we must beat into the ground to prove our worth.

Just another test that we must pass to gain our success.

Because success isn't your right,

You must fight

With all your grit and might

Make it through the night and shine your massive light on the world.

And show everyone you are a star.

Chapter 27:

4 Ways to Deal with Feelings of Inferiority When Comparing To Others

When we're feeling inferior, it's usually a result of comparing ourselves to other people and feeling like we don't measure up. And let's be real, it happens all. The. Damn. Time. You could be scrolling through your Instagram feed, notice a new picture of someone you follow, and think: *Wow, how do they always look so perfect?! No amount of filters will make me look like that!* Or maybe you show up to a party, and you quickly realize you're in a room full of accomplished people with exciting lives, and the thought of introducing yourself sends you into a panic. Suddenly, you're glancing at the door and wondering what your best escape plan is. You could be meeting your partner's family for the first time, and you're worried that you won't fit in or that they'll think you're not good enough. You might feel easily intimidated by other people and constantly obsess over what they think of you, even though it's beyond your control.

Don't worry! We have some coping strategies for you that will help you work through your feelings. Try 'em out and see for yourself!

1. Engage In Compassionate Self-Talk

When we feel inferior, we tend to pick ourselves apart and be hard on ourselves. Don't fall into the trap of being your own worst critic! Instead, build your <u>self-confidence</u> and self-esteem by saying positive things to yourself that resonate with you: *I'm feeling inferior right now, but I know my worth. I'm not defined by my credentials, my possessions, or my appearance. I am whole.*

2. Reach Out For Support Or Connect With A Friend

Just like the Beatles song goes: *I get by with a little help from my friends!* Reach out to someone you can trust and who will be there for you. You might feel inferior now, but it doesn't mean you have to navigate it alone! Get all of those negative feelings off your chest. Having someone there to validate our feelings can be so helpful!

3. Give Yourself A Pep Talk And Utilize A Helpful Statement

Comparing ourselves to other people just brings down our mood and makes us feel like garbage. Sometimes, we gotta give ourselves a little pep talk to turn those negative thoughts around. *I feel inferior right now, but I can get through this! I'm not the only person who has felt this way, and I won't be the last. Everything is gonna be okay!*

4. Comfort Yourself Like A Friend

If you don't have anyone who can be there for you at this moment, that's okay. You can be there for yourself! Think about how you would want a loved one to comfort you at this moment. Pat yourself on the back, treat yourself to some junk food, cuddle up on the couch with a warm, fuzzy blanket and binge your favorite show on Netflix. Be the friend you need right now!

Chapter 28:

Be Consistent, Not Perfect

It's often drilled into our heads that we have to be **great** at everything we do. It sounds like a lot of pressure, right? Well, what if the key wasn't in being great but simply showing up all the time, over and over?

Lasting progress isn't about being consistently great; it's about being great at being consistent. That means, instead of focusing on doing things perfectly, you simply focus on just the doing and getting better as you progress. When we focus on being consistent, <u>we give ourselves more of an opportunity for greatness</u>.

We're constantly seeing others online who are seemingly achieving greatness overnight—leaving us feeling stuck. But what if i told you that the true power is in the process?

When we aim for consistency over perfection, these are the benefits:

1. You're Taken More Seriously By Those Around You

You can tell people until you're blue in the face what you **want** to do, but if you don't do it, they'll stop listening. However, if you show up every day and make a consistent effort, you'll be synonymous with what you're putting out there. Others will see from your actions that you're passionate about what you do or believe in.

2. You'll Make Progress

How many times have you prolonged doing something until it became practically nonexistent because you kept waiting for it to be perfect? It was a hard pill to swallow, but i found out that my <u>fear archetype</u> was the procrastinator a few months ago. I've always considered myself a perfectionist, and i find out procrastination is one of our key traits. We tweak things repeatedly, hoping to make them perfect, and end up never actually taking action. When we show up consistently, despite how perfect something may or may not be, we increase the possibility of progress.

By bringing more consistency into our lives, we'll have the opportunity to see true change in our circumstances. When we harp on perfection, it can often stunt our ability to grow. So, how do you become more consistent?

First, understand that you might mess up. And that's okay.
The biggest thing holding us back from being more consistent and instead relying on perfection is that we're afraid of making mistakes.

When we mess up, we feel discouraged, and a way of protecting ourselves is by trying to control the outcome. So we wait until the time is perfect instead of taking the risk.

Allow yourself the space to be brave with your life. When faced with that fear, remind yourself that it's okay to make mistakes. To help, try reciting mantras like, "i may stumble, but i'll continue to learn and get better along the way."

A Small Step Is Always Better Than No Step At All

The most beneficial thing we can do for ourselves if we ever want to see change is to take action. Whether big or small, you are putting yourself out there, and doing the work consistently adds up. When we settle into the comfort of perfection, we stifle our potential.
So today or tomorrow, take one small action that will help move you in the direction you seek. And after that, do another small thing.
Along the way, praise your small wills and honor your process. With time and a steady effort, the things you desire will begin to manifest themselves.

Chapter 29:

Be Motivated by Challenge

You have an easy life and a continuous stream of income, you are lucky! You have everything you and your children need, you are lucky! You have your whole future planned ahead of you and nothing seems to go in the other direction yet, you are lucky!

But how far do you think this can go? What surety can you give yourself that all will go well from the start to the very end?

Life will always have a hurdle, a hardship, a challenge, right there when you feel most satisfied. What will you do then?

Will you give up and look for an escape? Will you seek guidance? Or will you just give up and go down a dark place because you never thought something like this could happen to you?

Life is full of endless possibilities and an endless parade of challenges that make life no walk in the park.

You are different from any other human being in at least one attribute. But your life isn't much different than most people's. You may be less fortunate, or you may be the luckiest, but you must not back down when life strikes you.

This world is a cruel place and a harsh terrain. But that doesn't mean you should give up whenever you get hit in the back. That doesn't mean you don't catch what the world throws at you.

Do you know what you should do? Look around and observe for examples. Examples of people who have had the same experiences as you had and what good or bad things did they do? You will find people on both extremes.

You will find people who didn't have the courage or guts to stand up to the challenge and people who didn't have the time to give up but to keep pushing harder and harder, just to get better at what they failed the last time.

The challenges of life can never cross your limits because the limits of a human being are practically infinite. But what feels like a heavy load, is just a shadow of your inner fear dictating you to give up.

But you can't give up, right? Because you already have what you need to overcome this challenge too. You just haven't looked into your backpack of skills yet!

If you are struggling at college, go out there and prove everyone in their wrong. Try to get better grades by putting in more hours little by little.

If people take you as a non-social person, try to talk to at least one new person each day.

If you aren't getting good at a sport, get tutorials and try to replicate the professionals' step by step and put in all your effort and time if you truly care for the challenge at hand.

The motivation you need is in the challenge itself. You just need to realize the true gains you want from each stone in your path, and you will find treasures under every stone.

Chapter 30:

Believe in Yourself

Listen up. I want to tell you a story. This story is about a boy. A boy who became a man, despite all odds. You see, when he was a child, he didn't have a lot going for him. The smallest and weakest in his class, he had to struggle every day just to keep up with his peers. Every minute of every hour was a fight against an opponent bigger and stronger than he was - and every day he was knocked down. Beaten. Defeated. But... despite that... despite everything that was going against him... this small, weak boy had one thing that separated him from hundreds of millions of people in this world. A differentiating factor that made a difference in the matter of what makes a winner in this world of losers. You see this boy believed in himself. No matter the odds, he believed fundamentally that he had the power to overcome anything that got in his way! It didn't matter how many times he was knocked down, he got RIGHT BACK UP!

Now it wasn't easy. It hurt like hell. Every time he failed was another reminder of how far behind, he was. A reminder of the nearly insurmountable gap between him and everyone else and lurking behind that reminder was the temptation, the suggestion to just give up. Throw in the towel. Surrender the win. Yet believe me when I tell you that no matter HOW tough things got, no matter HOW much he wanted to give in, a small voice in his heart keep saying... not today... just once more... I know it hurts but I can try again... Just. Once. More.

You see more than anything in this world HE KNEW that deep inside him was a greatness just WAITING to be tapped into! A power that most people would never see, but not him. It didn't matter what the world threw at him, because he'd be damned if he let his potential die alongside him. And all it took? All it required to unlock the chasm of greatness inside was a moment to realize the lies the world tried to tell him. In less than a second, he recognized the light inside that would ignite a spark of success to address the ones who didn't believe that he could do it. The ones who told him to give up! Get out! Go home and roam the streets where failure meets those who weren't born to sit at the seat at the top!

Yet what they didn't know is that being born weak didn't matter any longer cause in his fight to succeed he became stronger. Rising up to the heights beyond, he WOULD NOT GIVE UP till he forged a bond within his heart that ensured NO MATTER THE ODDS, no matter what anyone said about him, no matter what the world told him, he had something that NO ONE could take away from him. A power so strong it transformed this boy into a man. A loser into a winner. A failure into a success. That, is the power of self-belief...

www.ingramcontent.com/pod-product-compliance
Lightning Source LLC
Chambersburg PA
CBHW071125130526
44590CB00056B/2407